WHY?

A book with a question, and an answer, for everyone!

By Rudy Passaro

Dedication

I dedicate this simple book, with its monumental message, to my grandson Julian. Each of these questions examines a human emotion that can only bring sadness and woe. I have spent a lifetime trying to get to the last page and there is nothing more difficult. I ask God to guide everyone to the last page for the answer. Peace and happiness unto you Julian, forever.

Why do people fight?

Why are people jealous of one another?

Why are people mean towards one another?

Why do people hurt one another?

Why do people cause one another pain?

Why do people lie to one another?

Why do people neglect or hurt animals?

Why do people ignore those in need and allow them to suffer?

Why do people refuse to help one another?

Why do people steal from one another?

Why do people give up hope?

Because they forgot to..........

....

....

....

....

●●●●●●●●●●●●●●●●●●●●●●●●●

...LOVE!

God bless you!

Below, list which question was the most difficult to answer and explain why.

_____

_____

_____

_____

Draw a picture about your answer.

Use the next few pages to ask your own questions and draw your own pictures.

Why _____

_____

_____

_____

Why _____

_____

_____

_____

Why _____

_____

_____

_____

Why _____

_____

_____

_____

Why _____

_____

_____

_____

Why _____

_____

_____

_____

Now go out and talk to your friends and relatives about these questions. Compare your pictures and answers!

Made in the USA
Middletown, DE
13 November 2020